SCHOOL

That's Gross!
A Look at Science

Julie Murray

Big Buddy BOOKS
That's Gross!

VISIT US AT
www.abdopublishing.com

Published by ABDO Publishing Company, 8000 West 78th Street, Edina, Minnesota 55439.

Printed in the United States.

Coordinating Series Editor: Rochelle Baltzer
Editor: Sarah Tieck
Contributing Editor: Marcia Zappa
Graphic Design: Deborah Coldiron
Cover Photograph: *iStockPhoto:* iStockPhoto, Michal Rozanski; *Photos.com:* Jupiter Images.
Interior Photographs/Illustrations: *iStockPhoto:* Carlos Alvarez (p. 14), Aruind Balaraman (p. 29), Joshua Blake (p. 5), Jani Bryson (pp. 8, 20, 24), Jacek Chabraszewski (p. 26), David Dang (p. 5), Merrill Dyck (p. 12), Rob Friedman (p. 15), Sandra Henderson (p. 19), David Hernandez (p. 30), iStockPhoto (p. 9, 21, 27), Bonnie Jacobs (pp. 11, 23), Bela Tibor Kozma (p. 18), Rich Legg (p. 11), Hector Joseph Lumang (p. 21), Michelle Malven (p. 23), Georgy Markov (p. 21), Liza McCorkle (p. 13), Vasko Miokovic (p. 21), Nicholas Monu (p. 23, 30), Julian Rovagnati (p. 29), Michal Rozanski (p. 17), Jorge Salcedo (p. 29), Jordan Shaw (p. 25), Mike Sonnenberg (p. 17, 28), Sami Suni (p. 5); *Peter Arnold, Inc.:* CDC (p. 11), Michelle Del Guercio (p. 17), Darlyne A. Murawski (p. 7); *Photos.com:* Jupiter Images (pp. 5, 6, 7, 18).

Library of Congress Cataloging-in-Publication Data

Murray, Julie, 1969-
  School / Julie Murray.
     p. cm. -- (That's gross! A look at science)
  ISBN 978-1-60453-557-0
  1. Sanitary microbiology--Juvenile literature. 2. School hygiene--Juvenile literature. I. Title.

  QR48.M87 2009
  371.7'1--dc22
                                 2008039217

Contents

Exploring School

Your school is amazing! Learning happens. Friendships start. And, students grow and change.

Look a little closer. You'll see that behind all that cool stuff is a lot of yuck. Some of it is natural. Some of it is unhealthy. Let's explore!

Creepy Crawlies

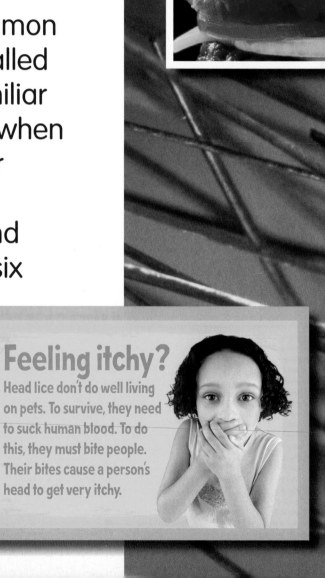

Schools are one of the most common spreading grounds for tiny bugs called head lice. You may already be familiar with head lice. They spread easily when classmates share hats, brushes, or headphones.

Head lice like to crawl around and nestle in people's hair. They have six legs and small claws. This helps them hold on to pieces of hair. Head lice cannot fly or jump.

Feeling itchy?

Head lice don't do well living on pets. To survive, they need to suck human blood. To do this, they must bite people. Their bites cause a person's head to get very itchy.

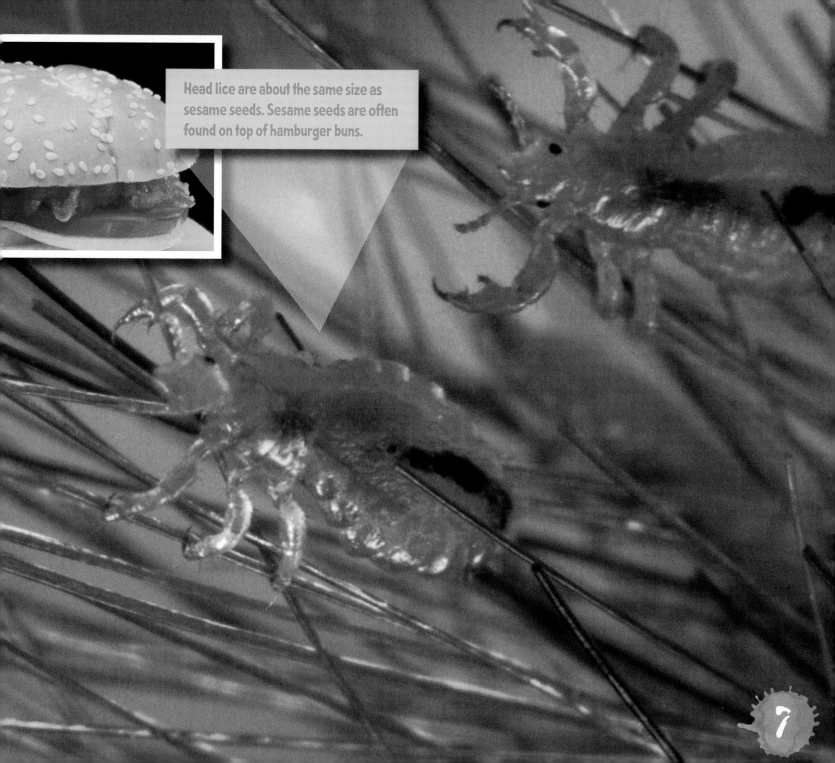

Head lice are about the same size as sesame seeds. Sesame seeds are often found on top of hamburger buns.

Head lice lay eggs called nits. The mother louse sticks her nits to a person's hair. Baby lice are called nymphs (NIHMFS). Nymphs are born every one to two weeks.

Most head lice live about 30 days on a person's head. During this time, a female might lay more than 100 eggs! If untreated, more lice will be born!

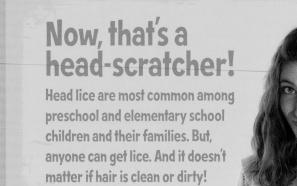

Now, that's a head-scratcher!

Head lice are most common among preschool and elementary school children and their families. But, anyone can get lice. And it doesn't matter if hair is clean or dirty!

Head lice can survive away from a human body for about two days.

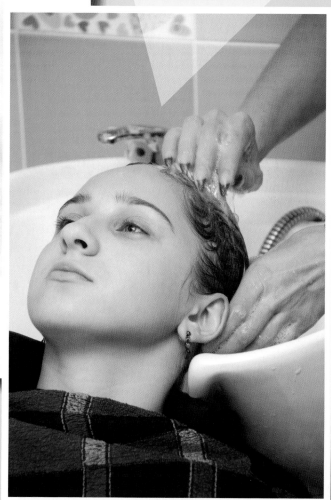

People use special shampoo to kill head lice, nits, and nymphs.

Germ Party

In school, lots of things are shared. That means there are many opportunities for **germs** (JUHRMS) to spread.

Germs are very small living things. The four types of germs are **bacteria** (bak-TIHR-ee-uh), viruses, fungi, and protozoa. They sneak into your body and make you sick.

When you touch doorknobs and pencils, you pick up germs. And, desks and keyboards are crawling with them. Gross!

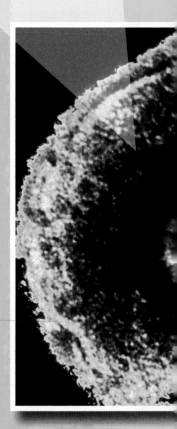

Bacteria can cause sore throats. Chicken pox is caused by a virus (*below*). Fungi can cause skin to be itchy, red, and cracked. Protozoa can give you runny poop!

10

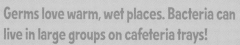
Germs love warm, wet places. Bacteria can live in large groups on cafeteria trays!

Scientists have found more germs on keyboards than toilet seats!

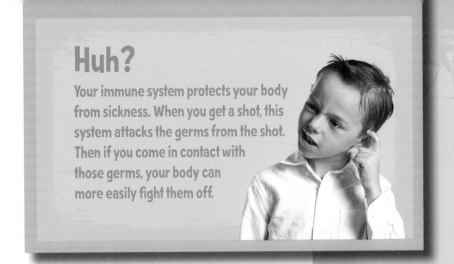

Huh?

Your immune system protects your body from sickness. When you get a shot, this system attacks the germs from the shot. Then if you come in contact with those germs, your body can more easily fight them off.

Germs aren't always bad, though. Some germs are used to keep you healthy.

Very small amounts of certain germs are inside a shot. When you get a shot, a needle pushes these germs inside your body. The small amount of germs help you fight off larger germs and stay healthy.

Using germs to help people stay healthy is called immunization (ih-myuh-nuh-ZAY-shuhn). All students get immunization shots before attending school.

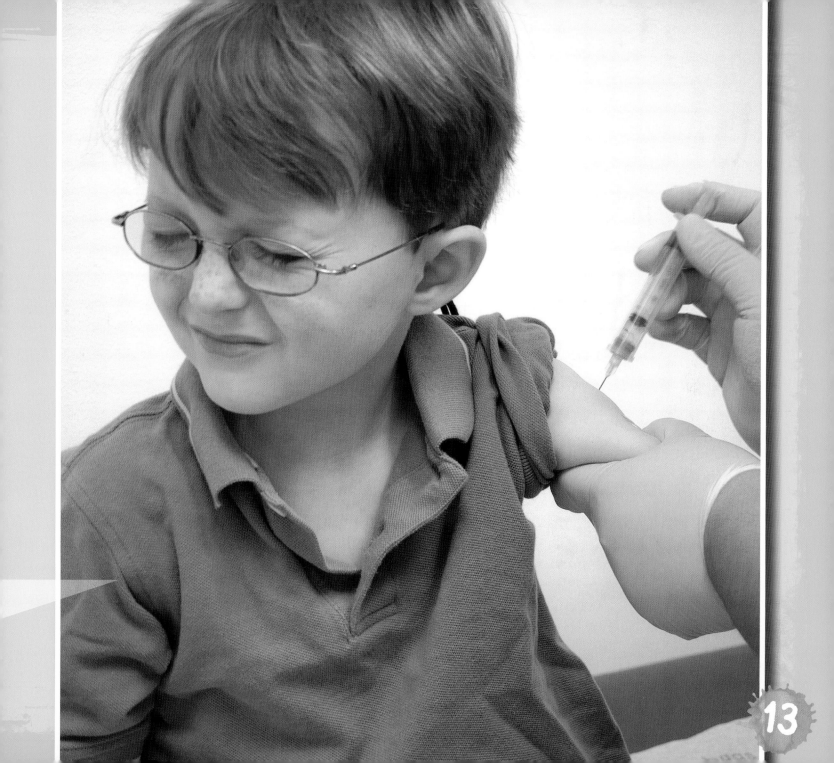

13

Want a Drink?

People slurp, cough, and spit when getting water at drinking fountains. Wads of gum and slimy boogers get stuck in the drain. And, sometimes people put their lips too close or sneeze on the spigot (SPIH-guht)! Eeeeww!

Because drinking fountains stay wet, germs can easily grow there. Some scientists believe they're the germiest spots in school!

No worries!

Despite the germs, drinking fountains are usually safe. Let the water run for 15 seconds before taking a drink. This helps clean off germs.

One study found more than 2 million bacteria per inch on a drinking fountain spigot!

Gooey Eyes

Pinkeye is another common sickness spread around the classroom. Pinkeye makes your eye look red. When you blink, it feels like sand is beneath your eyelid. And, gunk glues your eyes closed while you sleep.

This ooey, gooey sickness spreads fast! You can get it by touching someone or something **infected** with pinkeye and then touching your eye. And, you can even spread it from one of your eyes to the other!

The scientific name for pinkeye is conjunctivitis (kuhn-juhng-tih-VEYE-tuhs). That's because pinkeye affects the clear layer over the white of the eye. It is called the conjunctiva.

Did you know?

Allergies and matter in the eye can also cause pinkeye. These types of pinkeye are not spread by contact.

It's Alive!

Having a lot of homework might seem pretty gross. But, you'll find many yuckier things hiding in your locker!

The bottom of your backpack can be as dirty as your shoe! It is put on the floor, the playground, and other surfaces. Everywhere it goes, it picks up dirt and **germs**. Yuck!

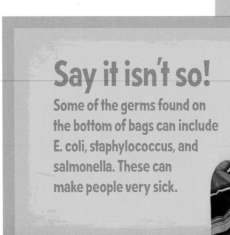

Say it isn't so!

Some of the germs found on the bottom of bags can include E. coli, staphylococcus, and salmonella. These can make people very sick.

Your backpack is likely very germy. And, so are your school supplies! You probably touch germy things, such as doorknobs or desks, before handling your school supplies.

Remember that lunch bag you threw in the back of your locker last week? If you open it, you might find some nasty-looking food.

Food can become unsafe to eat if it sits out too long. Fuzzy white and green molds sometimes grow on rotting food. Molds are very small living things. They give off spores that spread and grow more mold!

If food looks moldy, don't eat it. It can give you an upset stomach, a fever, or runny poop!

Molds don't just live on the surface of food. They have roots and branches. Molds are like very small threads throughout the food.

Molds can grow on other surfaces, too. This includes cloth, paper, and even wood (*below*)!

Smell My Feet

When you take off your shoes after gym class, watch out! Sweaty shoes and socks are wet and stinky.

Parts of your skin called **glands** make sweat. Each foot has more than 250,000 of them! They create a lot of moisture.

But, the sweat itself is not smelly. Sweat is almost all water from your body. **Bacteria** is what makes your feet smell.

Bacteria love dark, damp places. That's why so many live in your socks and shoes! They eat foot sweat. Then, they let out stinky waste. That's what smells so bad!

23

Digging for Gold?

Take cover when a classmate sneezes! Noses are fountains of gross stuff! They're full of snot and boogers. Snot is **mucus** (MYOO-kuhs). Sticky mucus catches dirt, **germs**, and pollution in the air. It keeps them out of your **lungs**. And, it helps protect your body from sickness. Boogers are made of dried snot, dirt, and germs. Picking your nose spreads the germs the mucus has collected.

Eeeeww!

Have you ever seen other students eating their boogers? Eating boogers brings all the germs and dirt from that mucus into the body. Yuck!

Your nose makes about one cup (.2 L) of snot each day!

Your nose uses powerful **muscles** (MUH-suhls) to push bad things out of your body. Sneezing uses your stomach, chest, and throat muscles. Even the muscles in your eyelids are involved! That is why your eyes sometimes close when you sneeze.

Sneezing is good, because it gets **mucus** and **germs** out of your body. But if you don't cover your mouth, snot and slobber will spray all over.

That WAS Gross!

Between head lice, gooey boogers, and super stinky feet, some very yucky things are at your school!

Now that you know about all the grossness, take a closer look. Many gross things are just a part of life and no big deal. Others can be prevented. Do what you can to live in a healthy way!

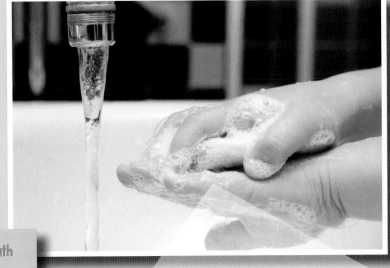

Be sure to cover your mouth when you cough or sneeze. If there's no tissue, use your upper arm. This keeps germs off your hands.

Washing hands helps keep away germs. Wash your hands for 20 to 30 seconds. To measure time, sing "Row, Row, Row Your Boat" or "Happy Birthday" one time while scrubbing.

Sometimes it is good not to share. For example, drinking out of your own cup can prevent sickness.

Eeeeww! What is THAT?

Answer on page 32.

Important Words

bacteria tiny one-celled organisms that can only be seen through a microscope. Some are germs.

drain something that helps remove liquids.

germs harmful organisms that can make people sick.

gland a body part that makes things the body needs. For example, sweat glands let out sweat to cool the skin.

infect to enter a body and make sick.

lungs a part of the body that helps the body breathe.

mucus thick, slippery, protective fluid from the body.

muscles body tissues, or layers of cells, that help move the body.

spigot something that can be turned on or off to control the flow of water.

spore a small, single-celled organism made by certain plants and animals that can grow into a new plant or animal.

Web Sites

To learn more about gross stuff, visit ABDO Publishing Company online. Web sites about gross stuff are featured on our Book Links page. These links are routinely monitored and updated to provide the most current information available.

www.abdopublishing.com

Index

"Eeeeww! What Is THAT?" answer: a moldy bagel.